A BEGINNER'S GUIDE FOR TRIATHLETES

JUMP START YOUR JOURNEY

BY

DR. TEKEMIA DORSEY
CHIEF EXECUTIVE OFFICER, LEAD AUTHOR
INTERNATIONAL ASSOCIATION OF BLACK TRIATHLETES
(IABT)
CO-AUTHORS: JOY MILES, TRA' RICHARDS, KEISHA
RAGOOBIR, JEREMY GORDON,
HOLLY GRAY, KIMBERLY "KD" RICHARD, NIA RICHARDSON,
NATHANIAL RICHARDSON

A BEGINNER'S GUIDE FOR TRIATHLETES

Dear Reader:

There are many who begin the journey of triathlons and while many succeed, just as many that fail. Those who succeed are those that take the time or who have taken the time to understand the sport, the industry, and its many disciplines. There are some that succeed in training but fail in events, for several reasons. In the multi-sport world, you will come to understand terms such as DQ (disqualified), DNF (did not finish), or even DNS (did not start). What are the causes of people experiencing DQ's, DNF's, or DNS's there are a number that come to mind? There really is not a definitive answer for or against to pinpoint the correct answer for everyone however there are a few factors that are universal to all regardless of.......

These variables are important to people, the sport, and to one's success. In the multi-sport industry, there are very few books for beginner's that speak on the topics introduced in this book. This book is unique for several reasons, (1) it is written by all African Americans; (2) it is written by all African American Certified Coaches (Subject Matter-Experts); (3) it is the first book written by all African American Certified Coaches; (4) it is designed to lend a hand to begin your journey in the multi-sport industry and (5) it introduces topics that other authors who are non-African American cannot discuss or begin to understand. This book is designed for any individual that is interested in getting started multi-disciplined sports, who are African American, a youth, or fall in the category of Athena or Clydesdale. #HappyReading

Dr. Tekemia Dorsey
Chief Executive Officer, Lead Author
International Association of Black Triathletes (IABT)

TABLE OF CONTENTS

Swimming

How do I get started?

Making the decision to start swimming is not a fly by night decision. There are a lot of variables to consider. First, what resources are available in my community? Does my community have a Park District "Learn to Swim" program? Is there a local fitness center that offers Private or Semi-Private swim lessons? Once that decision has been made, make an appointment with the instructor to discuss the following:

1. Are you experienced with working with beginners?

2. What is your method of teaching beginners how to swim?

3. Would it be possible for me to observe one of your sessions or do a trial session?

4. Who are you certified through and do you have referrals that I may contact?

Some other considerations that you may want to consider:

1. What does my daily schedule look like?

2. Will I be able to get practice time in before my next session?

3. Will I have the support of friends and family in this venture?

How to overcome swimming fears

Swimming fears are real. Anyone who says that they are not do not understand the complexity of those fears. Overcoming fears are hard and at times can be debilitating, but they can be overcome. Some steps that can help overcome those fears:

1. Try to discover the root cause of that fear. Did the fear come from a traumatic event in your life? Did the fear come from a preconceived belief from a friend? A family member? Did or do you still have a fear of drowning?

2. Address the fear. Speaking to someone, say a friend can help you work through any issues that you may have with it.

3. Speak with your coach. Try to explore options that will help you overcome your fear such as relaxation techniques, such as breathing and or visualization drills. Another option is starting the lesson on the pool deck and then slowly transition to the shallow end of the pool.

The key here is establishing a safe space to overcome the anxiety and the fear. Even elite Olympic swimmers have expressed issues with fear and/or anxiety. Do not feel as if you are alone in this endeavor. But also know that some amount of fear is common.

Tips for success as a beginner swimmer
Some tips for success as a beginner swimmer is the following:

1. Practice, practice, practice. The drills that you learn from your coach are tools in your toolbox to help you succeed in becoming a swimmer-not a beginner, but a swimmer.

2. Have patience. Rome wasn't built in a day. Swimming is one of the most technical of sports. To this day, there are Olympians who are still refining their craft when it comes to swimming. Just one small change can make the world of difference in your swim.

3. Enlist in friends and other beginners to help ease that transition.

4. Have open dialogue with your coach.

Joy Miles is a Pilates Trainer with an active Endurance habit. In addition to being a Pilates Trainer, she is also a Personal Trainer, USAT Level 1 Certified Coach, USATF Level 1 Certified Coach, a marathoner and IRONMAN athlete. She is a lover of all things caffeine, Prince, and dance. When she is not racing, she is finding ways to inspire others to fitness, working with Team Bright Pink and Team to End AIDS Chicago, writing blog articles and cheering on others at races wearing her trademark tutu, afro, cup of coffee and a smile.

Strength Training

Triathletes are conquerors of many disciplines. With the time being spent running, cycling, and swimming, strength training often falls to the curb or even worse, is never included in the workout regimen to begin with. Well, as it turns out, this can leave a triathlete at a major disadvantage. In order to perform at the top of your ability, strength training should serve as the priority activity because it builds and conditions the foundational structure...your wonderfully designed body!

In addition to its performance benefits, strength training can also play an important role in keeping you healthy and injury-free. Swimming, biking and running, while great for cardiovascular health, have the potential to cause overuse injuries, such as shin splints, plantar fasciitis, IT Band Syndrome, etc. Proper strength training can prevent these injuries. Also, in cases when they injuries have already occurred, strength training can also help with treatment by improving the ailments previously listed.

Strength training (also called resistance training or weight training) is the use of resistance to muscular contraction to build the strength, anaerobic endurance and size of skeletal muscles.

Strength training is based on the principle that muscles of the body will work to overcome a resistance force when they are required to do so. When you do resistance training repeatedly and consistently, your muscles become stronger.

While fitting in yet another activity may sound like a humongous task, you can make yourself a better all-around athlete with a simple strength plan that takes approximately 30-60 minutes per session, 3 times a week. Not only can this make you faster, it will also keep you feeling your best as you swim, pedal, and pound your way to the finish line.

So.... I am going to present three different workouts that you can do anywhere, even the comfort of your home. The workouts consist of bodyweight only exercises but as you become stronger, feel free to add some resistance (dumbbells, water bottles, laundry detergent containers, soup cans, etc.). Also, these are full-body workouts so you will do each workout once a week, skipping at least one day in between.

All of the workouts start with a warm-up. You will be doing a combination of three activities in your warm-up so split the allotted time to incorporate each one. Warming up is critical because it increases overall body and muscle temperatures which results in an increase in blood flow to the active muscles. Soft tissue (tendons, ligaments, muscles) injuries are less likely with a proper warm-up.

Without warming up, dangerous stress is placed on the heart while including it reduces the stress on the heart. Lastly, there is a psychological benefit from proper warm-up...it makes you feel more ready to participate and hit BEASTMODE! ☺

Additionally, the end of your workout is equally important so you will carve out time to stretch, as this will also have the added benefit of cooling down your body. Stretching when your muscles are warm can improve your flexibility over time, which in turn, helps prevent injury. You should stretch every major muscle group after your workout, holding each stretch for 10 to 20 seconds and breathing throughout. Stretching should not hurt, but you should feel tension in the muscle being stretched. Simple yoga poses are great to end your session with. An example of a cool down routine using 5 yoga poses is Cat Cow, Child's Pose, Downward Dog, Plank, and Cobra.

There are 5 exercises in each workout. You will do 10 repetitions for each exercise and that will complete one set. After completing the set, rest for 2 minutes and then do two more sets including a rest period in between. When finished, you will have done a total of 3 sets. That is fantastic! That equates to 150 reps...some pretty impressive strength training!

The workouts are as follows:

WORKOUT 1

- Jumping Jacks/High Knees/Butt Kickers (5-10min warm-up)

- Squats

- Push-ups

- Fire Hydrants

- Spiderman Planks (alternating sides)

- Supermans

- Stretch (full body, 5-10min cool-down)

WORKOUT 2

- Jumping Jacks/High Knees/Butt Kickers (5-10min warm-up)

- Front Lunges (alternating)

- Standing Twists

- Side Lunges w/Arm Circles (alternating)

- Tricep Dips

- Burpees

- Stretch (full body, 5-10min cool-down)

WORKOUT 3

- Jumping Jacks/High Knees/Butt Kickers (5-10min warm-up)

- Inchworms

- Sumo Squats w/Shoulder Press

- Mountain Climbers

- Butt Lifts (Bridges)

- Russian Twists

- Stretch (full body, 5-10min cool-down)

Now, you can find descriptions on how to perform each exercise on bodybuilding.com, youtube.com, or simply use google.com. Start slowly and practice good form. For your first couple of weeks you will probably want to stay within the 2-3 sets range.

Depending on your progress, by week 3, you can add an additional set. Approximately every couple of weeks thereafter, review your progress and continue to add sets and/or some form of resistance.

In summary, all too many triathletes sacrifice strength training in favor of additional swim, bike or run sessions. Truth be told, a well-executed strength-training program can allow you to carve up to 25 percent out of your swim, bike and run volume while improving performance and enjoying better race-day results.

If you make the time to build up your lean muscle mass, your endurance volume will increase. In a race like the triathlon, where you will be pushing your body to its limit for a several hours, having the fortitudes to endure the entire race is important. Building up stamina through practicing each discipline can help, but it can really only take you so far. Stronger muscles will allow you to maximize your stamina and carry you for the entire race.

So train hard, find enjoyment in the process, and go out there and conquer your events knowing that the time and dedication in your preparation is going to pay off in a major way. Truly relish the fruits of your labor. After all, you are more than just an average athlete. You are a TRIATHLETE!

Tra Richards, Owner and Founder of Fit Girls Clique and Body Builder. Tra continues to take part in body building competitions til this day, all while enjoying family and friends along the way.

Cycling

The bike portion of any race remains the most difficult to master in multi-disciplined sports and remains the discipline that can make or break one's success in a race. Cycling is a sport that people should enjoy regardless of preparing for an event or not as there are many benefits to the discipline itself. Benefits of cycling include but are not limited to, it is a way to exercise; it is a way to travel to and from work; it is a way to enjoy family bonding time; it is a way to build strength, endurance and power, just to name a few. If nothing else, consider cycling as a way of life to enjoy daily.

There are many variables to consider as you jump start your journey into multi-disciplined sports such as triathlons, duathlons, aquathons, etc. A few of those variables discussed in this chapter include bike selection, bike training, bike workshops, bike gadgets, and bike gear. These are just a few topics that is needed to be discussed to get started in the sport. The content in these sections are not to be exhaustive in nature but enough to provide a basic understanding of what to look out for when getting started. Let's explore.....

Bike Selection

Engaging in multi-disciplined sports such as triathlons, duathlons, Aqua Bike, etc., do not have to be expensive at all regardless of the age level. The myth is that bikes such as a road bike, a hybrid bike, or a Time Trial Bike (TT) makes a person faster than the next person but in fact, that myth is false. What makes a person faster than the next is not the type of bike, but more so the person riding the bike. With proper training, proper nutrition and hydration, a person can be more than average during the cycling portion of an event.

Bike Training

Bike training is an important variable to success in the cycling portion of an event regardless of the event such as triathlon, duathlon, Aqua-Bike, etc. Training is one of the hardest components people take part in. A few factors that make bike training less than smooth in the beginning is getting use to sitting of the seat, lack of mental strength, learning how to ride on surfaces such as hills, flat terrain, etc. Factors such as these get better in time through consistency in training. Like anything else in life where there is an interest, time must be made and in cycling, the same remains true. You must set time in your schedule to train, so that you can build endurance, power and mental strength. Seat time in the saddle in important so that you can gain familiarity with the bike and what it feels like to just sit and spin.

Bike training can take place indoors or outdoors; the choice remains yours. Some people will only train outdoors while some people will only train indoors. There are many that will engage in both depending on where they live, what event they are training for, and flexibility of training in one's schedule. The latter of these three variables are probability the most important (i.e. flexibility of training in one's schedule). This variable (in my opinion) remains the most important because without making time in one's schedule between home, work, family, etc, training will not be able to take place and training opportunity will not be as frequent as it could be.

Bike training indoors should be take place on rollers or a bike trainer. The bike trainer can be computerized or non-computerized. The choice remains yours. A bike trainer is a piece of equipment that connects your bike to the trainer itself. A bike trainer allows you to train in the comfort of your own home. There are quite a few brands of bike trainers to choose from. You may consider taking time to research the best brand that works for you and your budget.

Bike Trainers

A place to consider the search is on Amazon.com. When searching on a site such as Amazon, simply type in "Bike Trainer" and a host of options will appear. Another great resource to consider learning more about bike trainers is your local Bike Shop. Local Bike Shops remains a good resource to learn and view bike trainers and their functionality in person before deciding to make a purchase. Bike trainers can range from inexpensive to expensive. There are bike trainers that will assist in virtual training on the actual course of your event, if this remains a desire. When bike trainer shopping, it is a good idea to have a budget goal in mind of what you want to spend on a trainer or to know with certain, the functionality you seek in a bike trainer. Otherwise, it can become a costlier experience than desired.

Cycling Indoors vs Cycling Outdoors

If bike training outdoors, consider a time that allows an increase in visibility if possible. In other words, it is best to cycle during daylights hours as you can be best seen by motorists more easily. When cycling during the day, consider wearing bright clothing immediately. Wearing bright clothing assist motorists identifying you quicker than wearing dark colored clothes. Cycling on the road you want to e seen all the time. Although there are cycling laws in place, cyclists and motorists can become easily distracted while out on the road. It is better to take the high road towards safety than the low road, injury. If bike training must occur at night, the same rule applies in being seen by the motorists. In this case, you may consider reflective gear, lights strategically located on your bike such as on the handle bar and/or near the rear. Lights used can be flashing lights, bright lights, or light that do not flash. Some cyclists even place lights on the spooks that do not flash on their front and back wheels. The choice remains yours.

Bike Gear

Bike training in regular shorts and shirts are an option but not necessarily the best choice. When taking part in training or in competition consider the proper clothing recommended for comfort, breathability, durability, and that remain budget friendly. Most cyclists that have decided this is something they have an interest in invests in cycling shorts and cycling jackets.

Below is an example of IABT's Women Cycling Jacket and Shorts. Cycling Kits (Jackets and Shorts) can be customized any way your desire with any logo, in any color, and any style. The samples show below were designed for IABT's Junior MultiSport Club. As you can see from the images and descriptions further down, there are places in the Cycling Kit designed to add nutrition and hydration, if desired.

Women's Cycling Gear (Cycling Jacket/Cycling Shorts)

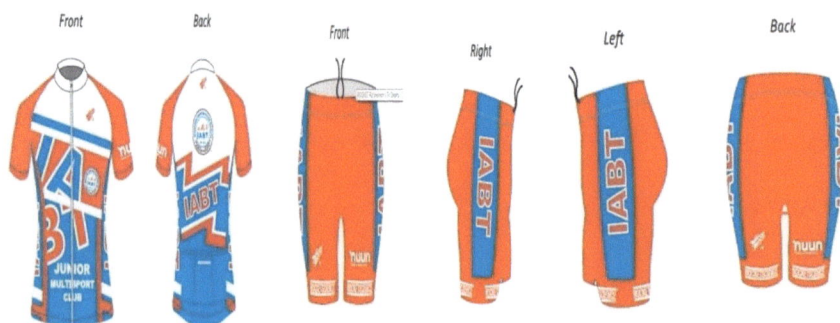

Women's Cycling Jacket (Description)

- LIGHT WEIGHT PERFECT FOR SPRING & SUMMER

- The light weight ROCKET RJ Women's Cycling Jersey with a form fitting streamlined fit, combined with aerodynamic seams results in a jersey that's truly made for performance and comfort.

- ENHANCED PERFORMANCE Overlock seams enhanced aerodynamics and flexibility.

- BREATHABILITY Fabric is extremely breathable and light.

- STAY DRY Ultra fine and soft 3D mesh Dry-Fit fabric helps keep you dry and comfortable by wicking sweat away to the fabric's surface, where it quickly evaporates.

- MORE FEATURES Signature silicone gripper at hem: Maintains fit. Full Front Zip for maximum comfort 3 back pockets

- UPF 50 PRODUCT DETAILS Fabric: Dry-Fit 100% polyester 3D mesh Machine wash Imported

Women's Cycling Tri Shorts (Description)
- The ROCKET RJ women's tri shorts are supportive and comfortable with the right amount of compression where you need it. Streamlined fit assures comfort and performance for all distance races from the local sprints to the full IronMan events.

- RocketTECH Chamois CLOSED CELL Technology, the first in the industry to reduce road vibration without absorbing water. Perforated with small wholes allow maximum ventilation and comfort, while they stretch and adjust to your body to promote comfort and eliminate chafing.

- ENHANCED MOVEMENT The fabric's high spandex content adds more stretch, creating a tight, supportive fit that enhances your range of motion as you race.

- BREATHABILITY Fabric is breathable yet with just the right amount of support even for the most challenging races.

- STAY DRY Smooth Quick-Dry fabric helps keep you dry and comfortable by wicking sweat away to the fabric's surface, where it quickly evaporates. MORE FEATURES Wide elastic waistband for more comfort Flat-lock seams feel smooth against your skin as you race SPF 50 helps you stay protected ageist the harmful UV rays 5 inch inseam

- PRODUCT DETAILS Fabric: Quick-Dry 80% polyester/ 20% spandex. Machine wash Imported

Solo Rides versus Group Rides

As a novice in the sport, be sure to take active part in bike trainings as often as you possibly can. Frequency and consistency in bike training will enhance familiarity with riding on various surfaces such as flat, hilly, off road, terrain, etc. Each of these surfaces require different bike handling skills from cyclists, so attempting to ride frequent remains beneficial.

Once you become comfortable with cycling alone and believe that you are ready to ride with others, then find a local group to ride with. How do you know if you are ever ready to ride with others you ask? Well, good question. You do not know because in group rides, there are various level of cyclists with various backgrounds (experience) and no matter how skilled you think you are, 9.9 times out of 10 you are destined to be dropped, have someone that is faster than you, slower than you, etc. When you are dropped during a ride, it simply means that you are not skilled enough to remain with the lead pack (cyclists) during the ride. Nevertheless, do not give up. Keep pedaling. Keep pedaling and keep returning to Group Rides to gain the experience and knowledge needed to take part in events such as triathlons, duathlons, aquabikes, etc.

Group Rides are beneficial to cyclists of all levels however you must have confidence and know yourself before venturing into group rides. Another benefit to group rides includes becoming acclimated with taking part in racing assimilation while training.

In events, you will be racing with other people and your job, other than knowing how to maneuver your bike, includes being able to ride with others in group formation. Other scenarios such as rules to road racing, drafting, passing, etc are also important to become familiar with. The goal in any event is to enjoy the event and to race injury free.

Bike Workshops

As a novice cyclists, you may consider engaging in cycling workshops as frequent as possible. Local bike shops often have trainings that are beneficial to you such as how to change a tire, how to clean your bike, etc. The more you become familiar with your bike and its components, the better off you will be. There is nothing worst then entering an event catching a flat tire and remaining on the side of the road for a lengthy period because you are unsure how to fix a flat. In addition to learning the components of your bike, it is important to purchase accessories needed in a case of emergency such as a spare tube, bike tools, portable air canister, etc. The more you know about cycling and the requirements of cycling safety, the more your confidence will grow and the more time you can focus on having fun as a cyclist.

Bike Gadgets

30

As a new person entering the sport, bike gadgets may not necessarily be at the top of your list of priorities. Bike gadgets are good for those who are seeking to enhance performance and endurance overtime and serves as a basis to understand, short term and long term goals. For example, let say you begin training and within an hour you were traveling 12 miles per hour and wanted to improve, as you become more comfortable with time in the saddle (training) you may consider a bike gadget such the use of a Garmin or other devices to track your Miles Per Hour (MPH). However, for just getting started in the sport, what is most important is getting acquainted with riding your bike consistently and remaining injury free.

List of Bike Gadgets to Consider

Bike Gadgets that may bring you joy and excitement over time are as follows.

1. Aero Bars

2. Speed/Cadence Sensor

3. Power Meter

4. Water Bottle Cages

5. Helmet

6. Sun Glasses

7. Bike Lights

8. Bike Cycle Computer

This list is not exhaustive in nature but designed to provide ideas on tools used to improve strength, endurance, stamina, power, FUN, etc.

Hydration Your Inner Cyclists

One of the setbacks for most cyclists is the lack of nutrition and hydration intake during training and events. As you begin to train more and eventually engage in your first event, whether it is a single discipline one such as a Cycling event or a multi-disciplined event such as triathlon/duathlons, etc., you need to ensure you have a proper hydration system in place. Hydration is a persons' and an athletes BEST FRIEND! Fluid intake in the form of water or another drink that replenishes the body such as Nuun, Powerade, etc should be a part of your system. H2O keep you hydrated and drinks such as Powerade, Nuun, etc assist in rehydration during training and events.

 Dr. Tekemia Dorsey is an award-winning business owner, award winning and best-selling author, endurance athlete, Ironman, marathoner, triathlete, duathlete, multi-disciplined local, state, and national level championship coach, and the only USAT Certified African American Female Race Director. She is a part of the Marathon Maniacs and the 50 States Marathon Club, just to name a few. Dr. Dorsey also played Professional Women Full Contact Football for the Baltimore Burn for 5 years and is the Commissioner of the Co-Ed Christian Softball League. She has been a certified coach on multiple levels such as high school, rec, club, etc since 1997.

Running

I love the sport of triathlon but running is my passion. To me there is nothing better than getting out in the open and hitting the pavement. Listening to nature, being alone with your thoughts or running with a group is a very freeing experience. To know that you are moving for miles on your own two feet to your destination to places where some people do not want to take the time to drive. Deciding to take on the sport of running was one of the better decisions I could have made. Not only did I become fit, I became more confident in my ability to do new and bigger activities such as doing 5ks, marathons and triathlons. It is an excellent sport but it can be challenging especially if you have not been active or not as in shape as you would like.

Tips Before Beginning A Running/Walking Regimen

So before you get started, you must ask yourself a few questions. You have to ask, are you ready for this lifestyle change? Are you ready to make a commitment to get moving and get off the couch even when you do not feel like it? Are you willing to put the time in to train even when circumstances not ideal? Do you have an outside support of family and friend and if not are you willing to keep going when things get hard or people, even love ones, do not support or understand your efforts? It is not uncomm n for friends and family to not quite understand this new thing you are embarking on, but that is ok, you just continue to set out to do what you have committed to. Another thing you should do is get with your doctor before you start any exercise regimen. If you have not exercised in a while, are overweight, have a family history of heart disease, or smoke you should see a physician before you start any routine. This way you can rule out any issues or answer any question you have about your health. It is reassuring to know you are in good health and also a good feeling that you are given the green light to take on the challenge of running. You should also see a doctor so that you can know your numbers. Many people do not know if their blood pressure or cholesterol levels are normal or if their BMI (Body Mass Index) is within normal range, this would be a good time to get a baseline and if these numbers are within or outside a healthy range you and your doctor can come up with a plan that can get these numbers under control.

Things Needed In Every Person's Running Toolbox

You made the decision to get off the couch and start running, now what? Beside a can-do attitude, what gear do you need to be successful. You do not have to spend a "mint" load of money to get started; all you need are a few basics things: a good pair of running shoes, wicking material shirt (not cotton), shorts or tights, ladies a good sports bra, non-cotton socks, and a water bottle. These are the basics, as you grow into the sport you may or may not want to add items such as a stopwatch or a GPS watch. Items such as these are nice to have but they are not a requirement for running. When shopping for running shoes, keep in mind that you want to get a good pair of running shoes that fit your run gait. Your running gait is basically the way your run (your posture, foot strike, etc.) and you need to have a shoe that will address any disparities in running you may have and help prevent injury as you continue the journey. Go to your local running store so that you can be evaluated and place in the proper run shoe. Keep in mind your running shoes will be larger than your everyday shoe. As you run, your feet will swell and the larger size will accommodate your foot so that your walk or run is more comfortable. Now, I have to warn you the shoe that is right for you may not be the shoe you are attracted to. Running shoes do not always come with the best color schemes, as hard as it may be don't overlook the fact that the best shoe for you may be the most boring looking shoe out there but when you are on the pavement that will not matter.

The color of the shoe will not help your game or prevent discomfort it the make of the shoe that makes a difference.

When shopping for running, gear go for the wicking material not cotton. Wicking material is frequently associated with performance and technical style shirts. It is a type of fabric that is used in workout clothes that is designed to allow the body to breath, draw moisture from the body, cotton does not allow for this because it holds water and you will be more apt to chafe. The idea behind wicking material is to help keep the body dry, comfortable and cool by wicking sweat away from the body. Fortunately, wicking material comes in a variety of styles and colors so what style may be lack in your running shoe you can definitely show some flare in your running clothes. Cotton socks can hold sweat and make your feet prone to blisters.

There are also a plethora of running socks you can choose from, ranging from slight compression, padded, wool, and toe socks. Once again, I would go to a reputable running store in your area and speak with a knowledgeable store representative and get the right sock for you.

Last but not least we need to discuss hydration gear. Walking or running will cause you to sweat and it is important to carry hydration with you to replace any water you have lost. You can either use a backpack, hand held or a hydration belt. These bottles come in multiple sizes and you will need to try to out to see what size works best for you on your run. Many runners find the hydration belt to be their go to gear. It allows you to wear your water around your waist so that your hands are free and relaxed. Another benefit many times these belts have compartments where you can place your keys, phone or any other essential you may need.

Running is seen by many people as a solo act, something you do on you own but the beauty about running is that it can be for you to spend some time alone or in a group. There is no right or wrong both have its pros or cons. Most find that running in a group helps them achieve a goal. There is accountability with running in groups and having someone to "answer" too. When you know a person or group of people are waiting for you to show up you are more apt to keep your appointment with the group.

It can be difficult getting up early or showing up at a run after a hard day at work and having the accountability of a group run makes it's a little easier because you know someone is counting on you to show up. Running in a group is also safer, especially if you run early in the morning or later in the evening.

Groups runs also help you stay on track with training, they can keep you accountable with pace and distance. Knowing that you have a group will help you stay on track so you won't cut your runs short. You will also find that group running allows you to develop relationship with other runners where you can talk about your experiences and feelings with people who can relate to you. As I stated in the intro sometimes your love ones or friends will not understand or cannot relate when you need to go for a run, which is where a group run is beneficial. Like -minded people running together for the same or different reason but you are running! Although running in a group is a good thing, running solo also has it benefits; it can be a great meditative experience just you, your thoughts and the pavement. This can also be a time where you can truly listen to your body, breathing, form and pace and be in competition with no one but yourself. There is no one setting the pace you do your thing. If you want to stop and walk you can do that. If you want to take a break and sit for a spell you can do that. If you want to run in a different location, you can do that unlike with a group you must go along with the masses.

You can all the tools, coaches and group runs at your disposal but in the end, the one person that will and should hold you accountable is you. You must be willing to do this even when no one else will be rooting for you or cheering you on one the side lines. You must be willing to do this even if you don't have the "best" gear that is being advertised. You must be willing to do this even when you want to just give in and stay in bed. When it is, all is said, and done, you are the best accountability partner there and you know what it will take to keep you going.

Keisha Ragoobir is a wife, mother, marathoner, triathlete, Board Member and Owner-Operator of Move4Word (M4W). Keisha is an avid pace leader, certified coach and personal trainer who has been featured in the September, 2015 edition of Runner's World. Not only does Keisha participate and places in races such as triathlons, etc, she can be heard singing the National Anthem at multiple Dallas races. Everything she does she always keeps her favorite verse Hebrew12:1 on her heart because she never knows who is watching.

Transition

The transition phases of a triathlon are when the athlete moves from one portion of the race to the next. Transitions are timed and as such are often referred to as "the fourth event." They are two of the most important and most overlooked parts of a triathlon. With training, knowledge and practice an athlete can make the transition phases operate in their favor instead of acting as liabilities.

The first transition will be from the swim to the bike; this is commonly referred to as T1. The second transition will be from the bike to the run; this is commonly referred to as T2. All transitions happen in a place called the transition area.

The transition area:

All transition activity will happen in the transition area. This will serve as the athlete's "home base" during a triathlon. The athlete will place all of their race items in this area: bike, helmet, shoes, nutrition, etc. Each athlete has a "bike corral" that corresponds to their number. The space for each athlete to place their items in the transition area is small; usually it is no more than three feet wide. The athlete will need to assemble their items in the

43

transition area orderly and efficiently in that bike corral. Failing to do this can result in a variable time penalty. *See USAT rule 7.2, http://www.usatriathlon.org/about-multisport/rulebook.aspx*

The areas where the athlete will start and end the bike and the run are connected to the transition area. The athlete must find out where they will "bike out/in" and "run out" and then remember that during the race for the best possible outcome.

A map of a transition area. Credit: http://trifreaks.com/federal-escape-triathlon-course-details/

<u>*Before the race:*</u>

Take time to find out where the transition area is on the course. If possible the athlete should try to find his or her individual bike corral. This should be available in the athlete guide in print or online if available, on the website or at packet pickup. If you are unable to find it at this point, ask a volunteer or the solutions desk for assistance.

If you are able to observe the transition area(s) before race day do so. The athlete should observe the size of the area and number of bike corrals. The athlete should observe the area where they will enter the transition area from the swim (the "swim in"), the area they will exit from in order to start and end the bike (the "bike out,") and the area where they will exit from to start the run (the "run out"). The athlete should also observe where their bike corral is in relation to all these places. The athlete should check with race officials and their packet to determine if they will need to check their bike into the transition area prior to race day and if so, when.

Nation's Triathlon in DC required bike check-in the day before!

Triathlete Guide to Triathlete Success – PACKING LIST

Triathlon Packing List

Swim
- ☐ Goggles
- ☐ Anti-Fog Solution
- ☐ Swim Cap
- ☐ Wetsuit
- ☐ PAM or Body Glide
- ☐ Spare goggles

Bike
- ☐ Bike
- ☐ Co2 Cartridges/Accessories
- ☐ Cycling Shoes
- ☐ Helmet
- ☐ Sunglasses
- ☐ Spare Tube
- ☐ Tire Levers
- ☐ Cycling Gloves

Run
- ☐ Race Belt
- ☐ Hat
- ☐ Running Shoes

General Items
- ☐ Towel
- ☐ Tri Shorts
- ☐ Tri Top
- ☐ Sports Bra/Underwear
- ☐ Socks (2 pairs)
- ☐ Race Numbers
- ☐ Flip Flips
- ☐ Post-Race Clothes
- ☐ Water Bottles (3-4)
- ☐ Fuel of your choice
- ☐ Flashlight
- ☐ Wrist Watch
- ☐ Vaseline
- ☐ Transition Bag
- ☐ Toilet Paper
- ☐ Sunscreen
- ☐ Money
- ☐ ID
- ☐ Timing Chip
- ☐ Bike Pump

ShapinUp.com

Setting Up Your Transition Area

Placing your items in transition in an orderly fashion is important for a fast transition time. There are many different theories as to his this should be done.

Some basics:

- Everything you need should be out of your bag/carrying item for fast access.

- The transition area is rather well guarded. I've never had a problem with theft at a race. That said, only bring what is absolutely necessary.

- There are certain items that you will need: the following is a list of what the triathlete would need.

- Your helmet is a good place to store things for the cycle and nutrition.

- Your water bottles can already be filled prior to the race.

- You don't have to be as dry as a bone to get on the bike.

- Don't bring any glass containers into transition. *See USAT Rule 7.5.*

There are many different ways to set up a bike corral. Possibly the most notable difference is the bicycle position. The bike can either be positioned with the handlebars on the crossbar or the seat on the crossbar. It is the athlete's preference in most cases. "The wheel of the bicycle must be down on the side of the assigned space." *See USAT Most Common Rule Violation #4, www.usatriathlon.org/about-multisport/rulebook/most-common-violations.aspx*

Triathlon transition area with handlebars on crossbar.

Credit

http://www.qwickness.com/?p=707

Triathlon Transition area with Bike seat on crossbar.

Credit

http://twotri.com/2012/02/beginner-triathlon-transition-tips/

The following, posted on Beginner Triathlete, is one way. Practice is the way to find the best strategy for the athlete.

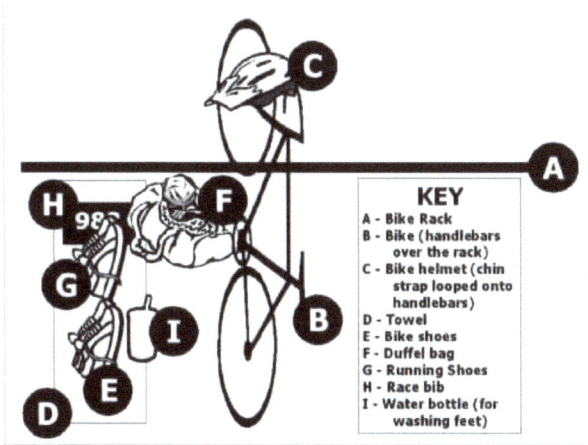

KEY
A - Bike Rack
B - Bike (handlebars over the rack)
C - Bike helmet (chin strap looped onto handlebars)
D - Towel
E - Bike shoes
F - Duffel bag
G - Running Shoes
H - Race bib
I - Water bottle (for washing feet)

credit http://www.beginnertriathlete.com/cms/article-detail.asp?articleid=115

An Example of a Transition:

The following is an example of the transition from the swim to the bike. As stated below, practice is the best way to get ready for transition and triathlon.

- Run/jog from the swim into T1. An athlete can walk in transition but remember that the clock is ticking. If wearing a wetsuit, try if possible to unzip the part over your upper body to prevent further bodily constriction.

Some triathlons have volunteers to assist triathletes remove their wetsuits. Credit: http://triforacure.org/swimming-guide

- If using a watch that is set to time your triathlon performance, press the button that indicates that you are changing events when you enter the transition area. See your watch's instruction manual for more details.

- Get to your bike corral

- Take off whatever parts of your wetsuit are still on if necessary. Place the wetsuit down. This step is skipped if no wetsuit is on.

- Take the helmet and put it on head, taking any necessary nutrition or sunglasses out of the helmet and in your suit pouches/on your head. Completely secure the helmet on your head before you leave the transition area, including completely fastening the chin strap. Keep the chin strap fastened at all times while on the bike. *See USAT Rule 5.9. See also Most Common Rules Violations #2, www.usatriathlon.org/about-multisport/rulebook/most-common-violations.aspx*

- Place your race belt with number on with the numbers over your backside.

- Use the water bottle to clean off your feet by squirting water on them with the bottle. Dry the feet off using the towel. Don't worry about drying off any other parts as they will dry naturally.

- put on your cycling socks and shoes. it's fine if a beginner wears socks with their bike shoes, but the athlete should remember that transitions are timed. Advanced transition methods include keeping the shoes on the bike clips, running out of transition and placing the feet in the shoes while cycling, but again that is advanced and should only be done with practice and training.

- Take the bike and run out of transition. Again, walking is permitted but transitions are timed.

- Do not impede other participants in the transition area. *See USAT rule 7.4.* An athlete experiencing problems with their equipment in the transition area MAY be able to get support from support staff or another triathlete either in the transition area or on the course but this is not guaranteed.

- DO NOT GET ON THE BIKE IN THE TRANSITION AREA. Wait until you cross the "mount line" near the start of the Bike course. The "mount line" is a line that an athlete must run their bike across before they can start cycling. Getting on your bike before crossing the mount line can result in time penalties and disqualification. *See USAT Rule 7.1 http://www.usatriathlon.org/about-multisport/rulebook.aspx*

a racer heads to the mount line while others who have passed it begin cycling. Credit https://joerunfordom.wordpress.com/2011/07/31/race-report-jacks-generic-triathlon/

- If using a watch that is set to time your triathlon performance, press the button that indicates that you are changing events when you cross the mount line.

- Mount your bike and begin the bike portion of the race.

An Example of T2

The following is an example of a trip through the transition area when transitioning from the bike to the run (T2)

- Slow down as you approach the dismount line. The Dismount line should be several feet from the beginning of the transition area.

- If using a watch that is set to time your triathlon performance, press the button that indicates that you are changing events when you cross the dismount line.

- Get off your bike before you reach the dismount line. A beginning triathlete should worry less about speed and more about a clean, safe dismount from the bike.

- Run the bike into the transition area. The athlete can walk the bike into the transition area but must remember that transitions are timed.

- Re-rack the bike in your transition space. Be sure to re-rack the bike properly or risk a time penalty. *See USAT Rule 7.3. See also USAT Most Common Rules Violations #4.*

- Remove the helmet and bike shoes. Some advanced triathletes remove their bike shoes while on the bike and run barefoot or in socks in the transition area, but this is an advanced move and should only be attempted with practice.

- Put running shoes and visor on. Place your race belt with number on with the numbers over your stomach. "All athletes are required to wear race numbers at all times during the run. Numbers must face the front and be clearly visible at all times. Numbers may not be cut or folded or altered in any way." *See USAT Most Common Rules Violations, #9.*

- Grab any supplemental nutrition or fuel belts from your transition space and run out of T2. An athlete can walk out of T2, but transitions are timed.

- If using a watch that is set to time your triathlon performance, press the button that indicates that you are changing events when you begin the run.

Transition Do's

Triathlete magazine has a list of do's and don'ts for the transition area. They are below.

- Bring a Pump. You could rely on the guy next to you, but that's not fair to him as he's trying to prepare for his race and is finding his pump pulled away every four minutes. Be self-sufficient and bring your home floor pump to top off the air in your tires on race morning.

- Bring Toilet Paper. You've stood in line for the Porta-Potty, made it to the front and entered to find no T.P. There's more than enough stress on race morning than to have to deal with the drama of having your wetsuit around your ankles five minutes before your wave goes off. Bring a roll in, and once you're done, leave it behind for someone else. It's a karmic pay-it-forward thing that everyone will appreciate.

- Keep Your Eyes Peeled. Folks dashing for age-group glory can move like a bull through a china shop, mowing over anything in their path. So keep an eye out for those overly excited competitors.

- Take your Time. Haste makes waste in triathlon transitions. What kind of waste? Forgetting to put your race number on. Forgetting to take your bike helmet off. That kind of thing. Pace yourself through transitions just as you do when swimming, cycling and running, to ensure that you get it all right the first time. If that means sitting down to pull off the wetsuit or pull on your shoes, go for it.

- Make a Pre-race Visual Cue. You've just dashed from the water and are headed into a sea of bikes. Where's yours? Be sure before the race to make a visual marker of which row your bike is, and how far down the rack it is. Some tie a balloon to the rack to mark their spot (though you don't see the pros doing this). Your best bet to find your bike is with a bright towel or transition mat—blaze orange, tie-dyed, the brighter the better.

- Keep a spare set of goggles. It's happened before: You pull on those favorite goggles and ... snap! The rubber strap breaks. Don't test the chaos theory; have a backup set in your transition bag. And if it happens to someone nearby, you can bail him out my tossing him your spare. You may be out 10 bucks, but you'll make it up in good karma.

- Practice. Before some Saturday bike ride, find a spot at the park and practice the transition procedure you plan to execute on race day. Bring a pair of running shoes and a towel. You don't need a rack; just lean the bike up against a wall and practice running up to the bike, putting on sunglasses and helmet and getting onto the bike. Likewise, set up an imaginary dismount line and practice safe, straight-lined stops and dismounts. It'll make your race-day experience a familiar one.

Transition Don'ts

- Move bikes to create prime real estate. Yes, that little space between the two bikes on the first rack would be perfect for your bike. If the owners of the bikes aren't there to ask if you can squeeze in, don't take it upon yourself to do so; these folks got in line early to get those prime spots at the rack, and they won't be keen to find that you've usurped the space. Move on down the rack and find an appropriate spot for your own goods.

- Overreach your rack space. With only so much real estate between bikes on a packed transition area rack, everyone needs only a bit of space to place his towel, running shoes and visor. Pick a spot to either side of your bike and claim no more than the width of your backpack for your gear placement. You only need enough space to place one set of bike shoes, one set of run shoes, a running hat and a race belt. Anything more is too much.

- Bring the kitchen sink. A disturbing trend at races is that folks bring not only their essential gear (a towel, race shoes, visor) but also non-essentials. That would include a dish bucket to rinse feet after the swim and bike, folding chairs. It's a race; leave the comfort accoutrements at home.

- Try new moves. Never done a flying mount onto your bike? Started a ride with your shoes already clipped to your bike? Done a rolling dismount? Don't try it on race day. These techniques save time when done well, but race day isn't the time to try them for the first time. Practice and perfect them in training.

- Forget anything. The best way to avoid showing up at the race, opening your duffel–A duffel? Really?–and realizing you've forgotten your wetsuit is to use a dedicated triathlon transition bag. They really do make a difference, with pockets and partitions for everything from wetsuit and run and bike shoes to keys and phone (so you're not on an Easter egg hunt post-race to call and tell your spouse about your epic day). There's a place for everything and everything's in its place.

Read more at

http://triathlon.competitor.com/2010/09/training/the-do%e2%80%99s-and-don%e2%80%99ts-of-the-triathlon-transition-area_12595#yFwcDJkb1PldoaAv.99

Different Transition Areas

Some races have more than one transition area, one for T1 and one for T2. While this is rare especially for beginning races, it is important to look for and take note of. This will be found by asking a race official, volunteer or observing the athlete guide. The athlete must make sure that each transition area has everything that they need for that transition. Planning and practice are necessary to complete these transitions appropriately.

Jeremy Gordon is a blogger, triathlete, duathlete, life coach, lawyer, and marathoner who love, life, liberty and the pursuit of happiness.

Nutrition

The importance of nutrition before to deciding to become a triathlete, during your training and racing and during recovery cannot be overstated. Your body has the best opportunity at performing at an optimal level when you are properly nourishing yourself.

The basis of a proper diet are macronutrients and micronutrients. Macronutrients consist of protein, carbohydrates and fats. Micronutrients are vitamins and minerals.

Macronutrients provide energy (calories). Not consuming the adequate number of calories from food to meet your energy requirements will result in a person experiencing detrimental changes to mental functioning and physical abilities.

Proteins

Proteins form the major structural component of muscle as well as the brain, nervous system, blood, skin and hair. In addition, proteins also transport micronutrients, fats and oxygen within the body. They help to form antibodies – the substance in our bodies which fight infection. Another important role proteins play is that in periods of energy deprivation, the body can break down proteins to use as a source for energy. Healthy sources of protein are lean cuts of meat, fish, nuts, seeds and soy.

Fats

Most people have a negative perception of fats. However, fats are just as important to the body as proteins and carbohydrates. Fats perform several important functions within the body which include but are not limited to, helps the body absorb vitamins, provides insulation and helps in hormone production. What must be remembered is that there are healthy fats (unsaturated and polyunsaturated fats) and those fats that are most often connected to an increased risk of health issues (saturated fats). It's recommended that your fat intake consist mainly from healthy sources such as avocado, olive oil, canola oil, water fish such as cod, salmon, tuna and mackerel. Another fact to note here is that essential fatty acids are a type of polyunsaturated fat that the body cannot produce and must be obtained from the diet. Omega- 6 and Omega-3 are fatty acids. These essential fatty acids can be found in egg yolk, avocado, flax seed, cold water fish and shellfish. For the non-athlete and athlete alike, the essential offer a variety of benefits including helping to dilate blood vessels and reducing inflammation.

Carbohydrates

Carbohydrates is another macronutrient that is often maligned by many. However, just as fats, carbs are a necessary dietary component. Carbohydrates are the body's preferred source of immediate energy and the only source of energy for the brain and red blood cells. When carbs are consumed in the form of fiber, they can improve digestive health and improve cholesterol levels. What needs to be avoided are the unhealthy carbs which include those foods that contain added sugars and refined starches. Instead choose healthy carbs – items such as fresh fruit, potatoes (all varieties), beans, fresh corn and whole grains (oats, rye, barley, quinoa and farro).

Micronutrients

While vitamins and minerals do not provide us with energy, they are essential to overall health and wellness. When choosing foods to eat, care should be given to ensure these food choices are nutrient dense. Nutrient dense foods and beverages provide vitamins and minerals which have positive health effects while supplying relatively few calories. In other words, nutrient dense foods provide vitamins and minerals but have not been diluted due to the addition of refined starches, solid fats or added sugars.

Humans need 13 different vitamins – A, BI, B2, B3(Niacin), B5 B6, B9 (folic acid), B12, Biotin, C, D, E, K. All but 2 of these vitamins are solely found in foods. There is no perfect food which contains these vitamins, so it's important that a variety of nutrient dense foods are consumed to ensure adequate vitamin intakes.

Minerals have a variety of roles to play and are critical for life. Some of the most critical minerals are as follows:

Calcium	Chromium
Copper	Fluoride
Iodine	Iron
Magnesium	Manganese
Phosphorus	Potassium
Selenium	Zinc

Nutrition While Training

Beginning triathletes will undoubtedly hear and read many things regarding what, when and how much they should be eating while training for their first race. Every plan and method will be as varied as the people offering their opinion and more than likely will render the "newbie" dazed and confused. However, after obtaining a clear understanding of the basic nutrition facts discussed in the previous sections, the new triathlete should have an easier time navigating through it all.

Training for a triathlon does not change basic nutrition facts. A well-balanced diet of carbohydrates, protein and fats which are dense in vitamins and minerals is key. A healthy nutrition plan and physical training go hand in hand. A bad diet cannot be out-swam, out-biked or out-run. So, the triathlete simply adds on to his/her basic knowledge of proper nutrition. The following will outline some guidelines which should be incorporated when training and participating in triathlon.

Remember that when the level of physical activity is increased by engaging in an exercise program or training for triathlon, the amount of energy (calories) the body requires increases. It's important to consult a nutritionist or registered dietician in order to determine how many additional calories your body requires. The number of calories each person requires is unique and based on a number of factors including – gender, age, height and activity level. The athlete needs to be concerned with the three stages of exercises – pre-exercise, during exercise and recovery (after exercise).

The primary goal of **pre-exercise** nutrition is to ensure that there is enough fuel/energy to perform at an optimum level. Foods that are relatively high in carbohydrates, low in fat and fiber (to minimize stomach issues), moderate in protein and are tolerated will by the athlete. The purpose of refueling **during exercise** is to provide the body with additional nutrients that are needed by the muscles and to keep energy levels up during long distance activities such as triathlons. When exercise lasts for more than 60 minutes, blood glucose levels (energy) begin to decrease and are down to almost nothing after 2-3 hours. (Glucose is just a scientific word for sugar). Therefore, it becomes critical to consume sugar containing beverages and snacks. A rule of thumb is to consume 30 to 60 grams of carbohydrate per hour of training (Rodriguez, Di Marco, & Langly, 2009). **Recovery nutrition's** goal is to replenish energy stores and to aid in the process of muscle repair. Recovery nutrition should be consumed within 30 minutes after exercise. The best recovery meals will include protein and carbs.

Protein and Triathletes

Because protein plays such a vital role in muscle strengthening and endurance exercises, it helps to optimize the athletic performance and the strength of the triathlete. Research shows that the effects of protein consumption are increased when taken around the time of exercise. Additionally, when protein is consumed immediately after physical activity, it helps in the building and repair of the muscle. There is no significant performance enhancement derived from consuming protein during exercise – especially if sufficient amounts of carbs are in the system.

The triathlete should also keep in mind that paying attention to how their body reacts to exercising or racing after eating particular types of proteins. For an example, although lean red meat is a great protein source, it may not be the best food to eat before a 3-mile practice run. Instead, opting to obtain protein through a less heavy source such as eggs, beans or nuts might be a better option. Depending on the fitness goals of the triathlete, a low, average or high protein diet can be selected. See table below:

Low Protein Diet	<10% of total calories consumed
Average Protein Diet	~15% of total calories consumed
High Protein Diet	>20% of total calories consumed
Very High Protein Diet	>30% of total calories consumed

Fats and Triathletes

Fats are a source of energy. Athletes, should consume the recommended amount of fats as the general population, which is about 20%-25% of total calories consumed.

Carbohydrates and Triathletes

Carbohydrates are very important for the triathlete as a source of pre-exercise and recovery nutrition. Depending on factors such as the exercise intensity & gender, the daily recommendation carb intake is approximately 3 to 5 grams per pound of body weight.

Holly Gray is the CFO of a real estate development company; a certified fitness nutrition specialist; mother of two and a lover of all things triathlon. Holly began participating in triathlon three years ago and since then has gone on to complete 15 Sprint and Olympic distance triathlons. Recognizing that nutrition was an integral part of maintaining her health and being a successful triathlete, Holly went on to become certified in fitness nutrition through the American Council on Exercise and received her certification in nutrition for endurance athletes through Ironman University. She is looking forward to completing her first Half Ironman and full Ironman-distance events this season.

Hair Care Tips for Triathletes

Sporty Afros was created in 2010 while Whitney Patterson and I trained for our first triathlon. Whenever we were in the gym, women (especially black women) would ask us what we were doing with our hair, what our training regimen was, how we were staying fit and looking cute, etc. We started a blog just to answer their questions, then realized there were limited resources women could go to find answers.

Sporty Afros is the first site specifically aimed to help black women achieve optimal health by connect the dots between hair care, exercise and nutrition. Since the start of the site, we have helped hundreds of women lose weight, feel empowered and jumpstart a healthy lifestyle. We love helping women figure out how to change their lives through fitness and nutrition and truly know that hair is a critical part of the process.

The "I Can't Workout Because of My Hair Excuse"

One of the biggest misconceptions or excuse we hear regarding women and their hair is that they can't work out because it will mess up their hair style. That's not necessarily true. We have tons of workout hair care solutions on our website. Another thing we

71

ask women is what's most important to them — their health or their hair?

Natural or Permed Hair Texture?

There is a big debate between being natural and permed. Both Whitney and I encourage women to choose what's best for their hair texture and personal preference. We both have trained with natural, transitioning and permed hair. Along the journey, we found it best for us to have natural hair and made a personal decision to do so. Again, our biggest focus has and is focusing on a complete healthy body rather than one aspect of the body. So choose what's best for you and consult with both your hair stylist and dermatologist if needed.

Items to Always Carry In Your Gym Bag

When creating your hair regimen for training, having the right arsenal of hair products and tools will ensure you can easily workout and not worry about your hair. Here are a few of products we recommend.

- Bobby Pins in various sizes

- Save Your Do Wrap

- Fedora or a head scarf

- Headbands of a variety of size

- Sample sizes and travel sizes of your favorite products

- A flake free gel

- Conditioner. Conditioner. Conditioner.

- Coconut and or olive oil

- Small studs

- Microfiber towel for your hair

I use a variety of products depending on our hair style and textures but some of our favorite product lines are Tgin, Obia Naturals, Giovanna, Beautiful Textures and Motions. We are often reviewing and researching other products so make sure that you check for more recommended products and lines.

Hair Care Tips 101 for Triathletes
On Sportyafros.com we have tons of tops but below are some of our typical hair care answers for triathletes.

- Always use conditioner or a form of moisturizer before swimming

- Protect the hair with a swim cap. We both love lyrca and spandex swim caps but there are tons to choose from including ones for locs and long hair

- Always rinse hair and body after swimming, unless practicing for an actual tri/brick day.

- Small twist, marley and low ponytails are great styles for triathletes but make sure hair is always secure and tucked away when engaging in an activity

- Make sure you keep hair cleansed and moisturized with a proper hair regimen

- Discuss hair regimen and activities with a proper hair stylist

- Proper nutrition and hydration are vital for hair growth and healthiness

Braids and Protective Styles Tips

When training, most women turn to braids, twist or some form of protective style so they can focus on training and not their hair. When wearing braids or weave, it's important to maintain a proper hair regimen as well. Make sure hair and scalp are cleansed regularly. Using an oil with a pointed tip applicator a few times a week will ensure your scalp and hair stays moisturized in braids or weave. Women shouldn't keep braids or weave than 8 weeks. After that point, hair can start to smell, matte. There is nothing worse than taking down braids and weave to find that your hair is a tangled and a complete mess.

I do not recommend micro braids or any hairstyle that are heavy and or may cause damage to your edges. Sorry ladies, but the weight of the water on your braids is a no-no. This results in damaged hairlines in a heartbeat if you are not careful. Box braids and twists are much more forgiving and easier on the hair if braided/twisted properly.

From a cute quick up-do to a faithful cute wig, make sure that you have a hairstyle you can do within 10 minutes or less after a workout. It's important to remove the hair barriers and frustrations while you're training to ensure your energy is focused on working out.

Swimming Specific Products

One of the most popular questions we are asked is the best shampoos for swimmers. These shampoos are perfect to clarify and restore balance to the hair after a long swim. Don't forget to follow up with both a conditioner and intensive deep conditioner to replenish the hair.

- Aubrey Organics Swimmer's Shampoo

- Nothing But Clarifying Shampoo

- Organic Black Soap Shampoo

- Ouidad Superfruit Renewal™ Clarifying Cream Shampoo

- Moptop Clarifying Rescue Treatment

Alexandria "Alex" Williams, is an internationally known FitHair and Travel Expert. She is a devoted lover of kale, neon, and Christ. As a Board Member of the National Association of Black Marathoners you can always find her running across a finish line or on her way to captivate an audience on the latest travel and communication news.

Image of Women In Triathlons

Training for triathlons are challenging enough without having the extra burden of being insecure about how you look. Sure, you are perfectly capable of performing well in the swim, bike and run portions of event. You are even thrilled when you complete the event, but oh, those finisher's photos! They have a way of diminishing your performance, don't they? What if it's your first TRI? Now you have to worry about your appearance AND your performance in all three events. Well, here are some things plus size women can focus on during training and on the day of the event to make triathlons a more confidence building experience.

During triathlon training.

Whether you have decided to work with a coach, in a group or by yourself using a training plan, you have to resist the urge of thinking "everyone is looking at me" or I bet they're thinking I'm too fat to do a triathlon". Get out of the mind reading business!! Instead, get into the habit of talking to people about your training. Ask your coach if he/she has worked with plus size athletes and ask them to provide references that you could speak with. Depending on your ability, talk with your group instructor before classes begin to eliminate any awkward conversations

77

about what you can and can not do during training. There's nothing worse than having to be the one the instructor makes assumptions about. It can ruin the entire session. When it comes to doing it on your own, get out of your comfort zone and post your training (good and bad), complete with pictures on social media. It will help to quiet the inner "fat chick" because you'll receive the loving support you need from family and friends. By race day you'll really be proud of yourself – performance and pictures!

The most important aspect of training for a triathlon is having control over your state of mind. During training, what would you prefer to focus on? Your belly fat showing through your swimsuit or those swim laps that need to get done? Four to six months of training can change both – the work is up to you. You can consult with a nutritionist to help you create a fuel plan to go with your training, so you eat just the amount of calories for your workout and still lose weight. (See Holly's section on NUTRITION) You can work with a trainer outside of your triathlon workout on strength training to burn fat and strengthen your muscles. (See Tra's section on WEIGHT LIFTING) Or you can choose to stay at your current weight and become more fit. But you control the choice you ultimately make, so no regrets on race day.

Clothing options for the plus size triathlete

The first thing you realize about triathlon gear is that it is not made for anyone over a size 12. Sizes such as XL and XXL or even XXXXL are extremely difficult to find or completely don't exist. Most often, plus size women are forced to shop in the men's sporting section just to find something to train in. Black, grey and red are usually the color choices and of course, none of it is close to fitting the feminine physique. Well good news! Brands are starting to respond to our need to have tri gear in plus sizes and they are cute both in color and in style. First things first, check the sizing charts and take your measurements. It won't matter how cute that tri kit is and how wonderfully it matches your helmet. If it doesn't fit, you are going to be miserable during training or worse yet, if you haven't worn it before race day, on the day of the event. (Huge mistake!

Have you given any thought to what makes you comfortable in clothing, in particular, triathlon gear? Is shirt length important to you? How long or short do you like it to fit in the torso? Are your shoulders broad? Do you look better in capped sleeve bike jerseys or a tank top version? If you prefer racer back tri shirts (The most difficult to find in plus size because of the built in bras) do you want to sacrifice the form fit for more room around the waist or risk getting underarm chafing? What about your cycle shorts? We focus heavily on whether we're comfortable with padding but what's important to you – long or short inseams? Do your shorts need to fit below the hip or look like capris? Do your shorts ride up and cause chafing? How about the waist on those cycle shorts? Do you like your shorts to wear at the natural waist or higher? What about the band on the shorts – large or narrow? There's nothing like a waist band that constantly flips over while biking or running.

Now that you have your measurements and the answers to all those questions, here's a great list of websites that cater to the plus size triathlete. Happy shopping!

Websites For Shopping
- www.aerotechdesigns.com

- www.teamestrogen.com

- www.swimoutlet.com

- www.cafepress.com (for t-shirts with TRI logos)

- www.swimsuitsforall.com

- www.junonia.com (their JunoActive brand)

- www.dolfinswimwear.com (sz up to 40)

- www.freecountry.com

Other Resources

1. Sports Authority, Dick's Sporting Goods and Lands' End (but sizes usually go up to sz 40 in swimsuits and other tri gear like cycling shorts are not true to size)

2. Old Navy and Lane Bryant/the Avenue online.

3. Walmart and Costco – for swimsuits and lycra shorts, skorts and capris

SHOWTIME – The Day of the Event

The truth is, you can do anything with the body you have right now. Plus-sized women are training for marathons, century rides and triathlons! In addition to age group categories, many plus size competitors are choosing to register in the Athena category at many triathlon events. You are ranked against women in your age group and your weight range. Typically, Athena is classified as women over 165lbs, age 39 and under and 40 years of age and over. You don't have to register as an Athena, it is an option and definitely a strategic move toward placing at an event. Think about it. If only 1% of the total population is competing in triathlons in general, how many plus size athletes, specifically females, are competing at the race you registered for? Can you say podium placer?! As you progress in triathlon, check the stats on races you participate in. For example, did you place 13th of 15 in your age group but would have placed 2nd out of 7 if you registered as an Athena? Unfortunately, many age groupers believe Athenas have an unfair advantage at podium placing. Expect to hear the efforts of Athenas downplayed on social media and in articles. Nevertheless, seek out Athena participants after the race and ask them if they are a part of a local group. You can also search Facebook or Google for online Athena groups.

Other things to consider.

Athena participants start in the last wave of the swim start. If you are a "slow" triathlete, particularly at the swim, you must be mentally prepared that the race organizers will be shutting down the course before or during your finish. If you are a middle of the pack type triathlete, you may want to determine whether the age group or the Athena category will give you the best results. If you're a fast racer, consider the USA Triathlon Athena National Championships. You could become the next Masters or Grandmasters winner! Weigh the pros and cons and make the best decision for you as a plus size triathlete.

Kimberly "KD" Richardson is a latecomer to endurance sports. A plus size mom of teenage twins, who is also an ovarian cancer survivor; she completed several races including a marathon and an ultra. As an Athena Triathlete, she is passionate about the inclusion of women of all sizes in this great sport.

Wisdom Shared from Seasoned Youth Triathletes – Part 1

1. *What does being a triathlete mean to you*?

What being a triathlete means to me is to always being prepared for what challenges you have in triathlons, and you should always believe in yourself and keep tri-ing. It also takes commitment. Sometimes I have to swim 4 days a week, and bike 3 days a week, but I know my biggest challenge is running. So even though I have to swim and bike so, much I have to make time to practice my running.

2. *Who is your role model and why*?

My role model is Wilma Rudolph because her leg got amputated and she thought she would never run again but she kept on practicing with the leg and she was running again and she was the fastest runner with an amputated leg. I know I am not a fast runner, so when I think about Wilma Rudolph it helps me to keep moving on.

85

3. ***How did you overcome your fears***?

I overcame my fears by just going for it. When I did my first open water triathlon I was very scared, because the waves were very, very big and they were pushing everybody in the water around. When it was my turn and I heard the air horn, I ran into the water and a huge wave pushed me sideways but I made it through the swim just fine. I always get nervous before every race, but when I get on the bike, my fears   go away.

4. ***What is your Favorite part of the triathlon? (Swim, Bike, Run)***

My favorite part of the triathlon is the swim because if it is a hot day and the water is cold, then I can cool off easily. When I get the chance to swim under the waves, it's such a great rush. When I swim in a pool, I get the chance to do flip turns, which are really fun. The one, thing I noticed between open water swims and swimming pool triathlons is in open water you only run into the water and start swimming but in the pool, you can use your feet to kick off the wall. I think triathlons with a pool swim go much faster.

5. ***Tips for aspiring youth- Triathletes***:

- Always train/practice.

- Always pack what you need for each part (Swim, Goggles, Race Cap and Towel, Bike, Helmet, and DONT FORGET YOUR RACE NUMBERS helmet and bike Run shoes and your race bib.)

- Always recheck your bag if you missed anything. And practice changing for each transition (dry off as fast as can and keep your shoes untied and loose so you can slip right into them, REMEMBER WHERE YOUR BIKE IS!!!)

- Just Go For it!!!!

- Always Believe in yourself!!!!

6. Which of the three disciplines is your strongest? Why?

I am a very strong swimmer

7. How have you been able to balance being a good triathlete and a good student?

I have been able to balance these two things because I mostly do my school work first. When triathlon starts, school is almost over. I usually do a lot of reading in the summer.

Nia Richardson, one of a set of 14-year old twins who love for triathlons and are outstanding triathletes. Nia started swimming at the age of five years old and progressed from Learn to Swim classes to becoming a team member of the Regional Swim Club for the Chicago Park District. Nia have a Black Belt in Taekwondo and is an accomplished violinist. Nia is looking forward to completing in adult races this year.

Wisdom Shared from Seasoned Youth Triathletes – Part 2

1. ***What does being a triathlete mean to you***?

To me, being a triathlete means to be disciplined, timely, and organized. It means that you need to plan ahead and that you need to practice. It also means have fun, be prepared, and be optimistic.

2. ***Who is your role model and why***?

My role model is Steve Jobs. He's my role model because he wasn't very popular, but he overcame all of his hardships and ignored everyone who told him he couldn't do it, or he needed to stop, and achieved greatness. He created one of the top 3 business enterprises that sell phones, computers, tablets, and more. I try to think like him whenever I approach my training. I learned from him that success comes from failing a few times and from being anxious to try again until I get right.

3. ***How did you overcome your fears***?

I never overcame my fear of diving. That's my only fear. I am still afraid, but I am taking steps so I can at least diminish the fear bit by bit. I can jump up and do the dolphin pose on the edge of the pool, but I am still afraid. I have to learn to dive because not every triathlon will allow me to walk in the water to start. *Like Escape From Alcatraz*, a TRI where you jump from a ferry that I hope to do when I'm a little older.

4. *What is your Favorite part of the triathlon? (Swim, Bike, Run)*

My favorite part of the triathlon is the bike. That's my favorite part of the bike because I really like riding bikes. Plus, I get to go really fast on it and I can do a lot of things on the bike, like wheelies. It's important to know your bike and all its parts too. There's fun in the bike and knowledge of your bike that makes training fun.

5. *Tips for aspiring youth - Triathletes*:

A few tips that I can give to future triathletes is

- Always be prepared. You need to make sure you have everything in a place where you can get it and is easily accessible.

- Practice. Make sure you can move very fast during the transitions, because the time doesn't stop for you to change clothes or putting your bike away.

- Don't overexert yourself. Sometimes, triathletes get too tired to continue just because they push themselves too far and can't rest. Make sure you get water and pace yourself.

- Take care of your things and bring extras. Sometimes, if your goggles break, or your swimsuit rips, bring an extra pair. That way, you can participate in the triathlon.

And most important...

- Have fun!!! The triathlon is a race and you don't have to be fast if you don't want to be, but you do want to beat your previous time. So it's up to you. It's your race, just be ok with your decision to train for it and what you decide to do during the race. That's all that matters.

6. Which of the three disciplines is your strongest? Why?

I am strongest at running. I run a lot and I am very fast. In swimming I am fast, but I still need to work on my form. On a bike

I am fast, but I need to learn how to pace myself on the bike. But running, my form is great, I can pace myself, and I am very fast.

7. How have you been able to balance being a good triathlete and a good student?

First, I made a schedule combining schoolwork and triathlon work. I did homework first, then go swimming one day, then do homework and go biking the second day, and then do homework and go running, then do it over again. That way, it doesn't interfere with my schoolwork, and I still have time to practice for my triathlons.

Nathanial Richardson, one of a set of 14-year old twins who love for triathlons and are outstanding triathletes. Nathanial started swimming at the age of five years old and progressed from Learn to Swim classes to becoming a team member of the Regional Swim Club for the Chicago Park District. Nathanial have a Black Belt in Taekwondo and is an accomplished violinist. Nathanial is looking forward to completing in adult races this year.

Selecting A Tri Coach

Swimming

Selecting a swimming coach

Selecting a swimming coach is like selecting a pair of good shoes. You want to be comfortable and that is the same in selecting a swimming coach. When selecting a coach, consider the following:

1. Is the coach a certified professional either through USMS (United States Masters Swimming), USA Swimming, Total Immersion, USA Triathlon or American Red Cross.

2. Do they coach beginners as well as experienced swimmers?

3. What is their philosophy of coaching?

4. Are they genuinely invested in your success?

5. Are you able to do a trial lesson or view a lesson?

6. Are you comfortable with the coach?

7. Do you have to purchase a separate membership to a facility in order to work with this coach?

8. Are you able to speak with current and past clients?

9. Get referrals from friends who have took private lessons.

These are a few steps in selecting a coach.

Cycling

You have plenty of options in selecting a coach for cycling such as a Certified Triathlon Coach or a Certified Cycling Coach. The difference between a Certified Cycling Coach versus a Certified Triathlon Coach is that the cycling coach will only focus on the cycling discipline which is a huge mistake in multi-disciplined sports. On the contrary triathlon coaches will focus on all three disciplines and how each discipline fits in the larger vision of the sport. If you are interested in cycling only, choose a cycling coach. If you are in multi-disciplined sports such as triathlons/duathlons, etc then the only choice is a Certified Triathlon Coach. It's just that simple.

Running

Before hiring a coach some of the things you should ask yourself the following: Can you afford a coach? You should consider not only the weekly monthly fees but also the travel to get to your sessions. If there is equipment or extra gear you need to purchase will you be able to or if there are additional fees that you may have pay such as gym or track use. Some coaches may include this in their service fee but it is good to know that up front.

Will you be willing to make the commitment or time sacrifice to work with a coach? When you enter into a program you have to realize that your time and commitment will be going in a different direction. Hiring a coach is a commitment and everyone's time is valuable so you need to look at your current schedule and ask yourself if you have the time to dedicate to a coach. If you are overloaded you may not be able to follow a program created that a coach expects you to do. Although your coach should create a program that is adaptable, it will still consume a lot of your time and you need to be ready for that.

What are your goals and are they realistic? Hiring a coach will help you get to where you need to be but you need to be realistic about what a coach can do within a period of time at your current fitness level. When interviewing a coach, be honest with yourself and your current fitness level; be as transparent as possible so the coach can honest with you about what they can do for you. If you want to train for a long distance race or triathlon and have not been active, understand that it can be 14- 16 weeks of consistent training with your coach to reach your goal.

Last but very important are you coachable? Once again be honest and transparent about yourself. Are you willing to listen to feedback from your coach that may not be as favorable as you like? Are you willing to do what your coach asks you to do even if you don't like it? Are you willing to trust your coach and the plan they set for you? Will you show up and put in the work?

We all know that everyone is not for everybody and that includes coach and client relationship. Both have to be able to communicate effectively, be encouraging, show up for sessions on time, adhere to contractual agreements and respect each other. After you have interviewed a coach and start to work together you still need to trust your instinct. If you feel something is not right address it with your coach, they should be willing to answer any of your questions that is within the scope of their certifications. If things are not working out between you and your coach it may be time to rethink your commitment. Just like a client has a responsibility to the program, the coach has a responsibility to their client and if either parties' are not able to adhere to the program or just flat out can't get along it may be necessary to cut ties and find a new coach. Before hiring a coach ask questions and review the termination agreement in your contract and make sure you understand it so if you have to terminate your relationship there is no confusion on what has to happen. As a coach, I communicate with clients weekly and I also have some ad-hoc conversation as well (note some coaches charge additional for any out of scope work). Conversations can range from training to about daily life and this is an opportunity where a coach- client relationship can grow and blossom but it can also be a time where either party can get a better insight if your relationship can work.

Tri Coach (Cycling, Nutrition, Strength & Conditioning, Swimming, Running)

Triathlons are a universal language that speak to everyone (young, old, fat, skinny, white, black, Baptist, Catholic, urban, rural, etc) and a Tri Coach is a coach that speak the universal language of triathlons (swimming, cycling, running, strength & conditioning, and nutrition/hydration), all in one. When selecting a Tri Coach, it is important as previously stated to ensure the Tri Coach is certified and it is extremely helpful if the Tri Coach has experience in events. There remains a gap between theory (becoming Certified) and practical experience (being a Triathlete). There are pros and cons to hiring a Certified Tri Coach versus being a Triathlete to guide/facilitate your tri process.

Certified Tri Coach versus Triathlete

Theory put into perspective; the nuisance of a foundation to assist in understanding each aspect of the sport, including how to run a business. A Tri Coach who become certified benefits from this type of training. While swimming, cycling, running, nutrition, and strength and conditioning are all individual disciplines, when understood collectively a Tri Coach is able to build a solid coaching program for their audience. Certified Tri Coaches approach working with triathletes from a holistic angle versus an individual one such as working with a single-disciplined Coach. A Certified Tri Coach also saves individual dollars on the cents in training costs and overall knowledge shared. Triathletes benefit from having a Coach who is familiar with each area of the sport plus additional areas.

On the contrary, theory is often tough to understand regardless of one's learning style unless experienced. However, experience alone is not enough to be able to discuss or lead another in the sport. Each triathlete experience the journey of becoming a triathlete differently such as training, goals, purpose, passion, setbacks, recovery, pros and cons. Normally, triathletes who do not hire a coach simply learn along the way from books, the Internet or from others they engage in conversation with. When working with triathletes seeking to either enter the sport or become advanced in the sport, experience as a triathlete is just not enough regardless of the level he/she competes on to train another properly. Theory forces an individual to guess what the experience will be like for its audience and because there are multiple disciplines in triathlons, knowledge acquisition can be extremely overwhelming, for even a triathlete who has experience.

Certified Tri Coach as a Triathlete

When selecting a coach, after you ensure (if desired) the coach is certified, then another criterion one may consider is for the individual to have triathlon experience as a triathlete versus a volunteer. Benefits of having a Tri Coach who is certified and a triathlete ensures that he/she triathlon experience and you know that what is being shared is sound, credible, and reliable. Now how much experience (years as a coach) and the level of experience (indoor; outdoor; pool versus open water; sprint, Oly,

70.3, 140.6) greatly depends on one's preference. Certified Tri Coaches are trained in both open water and pool training; strength and conditioning for the swim, run, and bike; trained to work with injured and overweight individuals; trained for bike fits; to work with power meters; to design a triathlon schedule to make the triathlon experience fit into your daily lifestyle as much as possible.

International Association of Black Triathletes (IABT)

PROGRAMS, SERVICES, PRODUCTS INCLUDE

▶ Training Plans
▶ Consulting
▶ Coaching
▶ Webinars
▶ Educational Materials
▶ Indoor/Outdoor Events
▶ Corporate Training
▶ Camps/Clinics
▶ Junior MultiSport Club
▶ Learn to Swim Programs
▶ Curriculum Developement
▶ Seminars/Workshops/Conferences

www.theiabt.com

INTERNATIONAL ASSOCIATION OF BLACK TRIATHLETES (IABT)

Website: www.theiabt.org   Phone: 443-267-8783

Email: iabtriathletes@gmail.com

www.ingramcontent.com/pod-product-compliance
Lightning Source LLC
Chambersburg PA
CBHW051233090426
42740CB00001B/3